Beyond the Grave

by L. C. Casterline, Mary Packard,
and the Editors of Ripley Entertainment Inc.

nancy hall, inc.

Table of Contents

A Necessary End

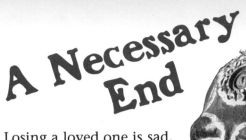

Losing a loved one is sad. You miss the person and grieve for them and know you will remember them all your life. Over the ages, people all over the world have devised customs and rituals to help them cope with the death of loved ones and found ways to remember them.

In New Guinea, many people kept and worshiped the skulls of their ancestors.

First, a decision needs to be made about the deceased person's body. Most bodies are buried or cremated. Many people donate their organs for transplants and, in a way, live on for awhile in another person. Some make

In Ghana, some people are buried in colorful, unusually shaped coffins, like this one of a fish.

arrangements to donate their whole bodies to science. A few donate their bodies to be made into art exhibits, while others have their bodies frozen and stored in the hope that someday technology will allow them to live again.

In *Beyond the Grave* you'll learn some of the ways people deal with grief and what they do with corpses. You'll read about mummies, shrunken heads, and unusual coffins, tombstones, and epitaphs—as well as ghosts, curses, superstitions, and more.

Cemeteries aren't all for deceased people. Pet cemeteries provide a place for people to memorialize their beloved pets.

Whether male or female, rich or poor, royalty or working class, death comes to us all—but with luck, not till after we've lived long, happy lives filled with love. So don't waste time. Enjoy life while you can and remember: Every day aboveground is a good one!

Rites of Passage

Everybody dies—but what to do with the body? How should loved ones honor and remember the deceased? There are as many answers to these age-old questions as there are deaths. Here are some of the more unusual ways people are buried and memorialized—in both ancient and modern times.

Masterful Mummies

No one was better at preserving the dead than the ancient Egyptians. In order to live forever, the Egyptians believed that the soul had to reunite with the body in the afterlife—so it was very important to them to have their bodies preserved. Poor people were buried in the desert, where the sun-warmed sand would dry out their bodies. The rich, however, were mummified.

A large gold mask, protected by magic spells, guarded the head of King Tutankhamun, who ruled from 1361 to 1352 B.C.E.

First, embalming priests removed all the organs except for the heart. The brain was removed through the nose and discarded. The stomach, liver, lungs, and intestines were washed and dried, then put into special containers called canopic jars.

After washing the body, the priests immersed it in several hundred pounds of natron (four different kinds of salt). There the corpse remained for 40 days, until the salt absorbed all the moisture. Then the dried body was rubbed with oils and stuffed with spices, linen, sawdust, and sand so it would hold its shape. Finally, it was wrapped in 150 yards of resin-soaked linen strips.

The finished mummy was protected by two wooden mummy cases, one inside the other, decorated with hieroglyphs and pictures of the gods. These cases were placed in a stone coffin called a sarcophagus, which was then put inside a tomb containing everything the dead person needed—from jewels to cooking utensils to pets—to have a fine time in the afterlife.

Cats, dogs, falcons, monkeys— even gazelles and crocodiles— were among the animals mummified by the ancient Egyptians. The 3,500-year-old mummified monkey at right can be seen in the Egyptian Museum in Cairo.

Mummies Around the World

Mummies have been found in many parts of the world. The Dani people of Irian Jaya, Indonesia, used to preserve the bodies of village leaders by smoking them. They believed the mummies had power and would give protection to the villagers.

In South America, the Chinchorro people were making mummies in 5000 B.C.E., 2,000 years before the Egyptians. The Chinchorros removed the skin, discarded the organs, and stripped the flesh from the bones. Then they put the skeleton back together, substituting clay and plant material for the organs and muscles. After stretching the skin back over the bones, they covered the

The mummy of a village elder in Irian Jaya

body with ash and black coloring, and often added a clay mask.

The Incas were still making mummies—and sacrificing humans—500 years ago. In 1995, Dr. Johan Reinhard found the frozen mummy of a sacrificed teenage girl more than 20,000 feet up on a mountain in Peru. To help keep her from thawing on the three-day journey back to town, Reinhard wrapped her in an insulated sleeping bag.

The mummy of a Tlingit shaman

In Alaska, the Tlingit people once embalmed the bodies of holy men called shamans and placed them in shelters along with the body of a slave to serve them in the afterlife.

Natural Mummies

Not all bodies are mummified on purpose. In 1972, two brothers stumbled upon a cave about 300 miles north of the Arctic Circle. It contained the 500-year-old bodies of eight Inuits, six women and two children, that had been preserved by the freezing-cold air.

Mummies more than 2,000 years old have been found in the peat bogs of Great Britain and northwestern Europe. Peat is decayed, densely packed organic matter that contains tannic acids, which weaken bones and soften skin.

A lobster-shaped coffin made by Paa Joe

Today, many people are buried in standard coffins picked out by their loved ones. Others, however, prefer to have their bodies tucked into something a little more special.

Kane Quaye Sowah of Ghana, began creating wooden coffins in unusual shapes, including animals, birds, vegetables, boats, and cars, in the mid-1970s. Each coffin was meant to reflect the personality, occupation, or status of the deceased. Sowah died in 1992, but his cousin and former apprentice, Paa Joe, continues the tradition today.

THEN

The tombs of ancient Etruscans were shaped to resemble the houses in which the deceased had lived.

In Chichester, New Hampshire, Down to Earth Coffins builds custom-made caskets that can be used as bookcases, tables, or even gun cabinets until they are needed for burial.

Some people prefer to be buried in their own wheels. In 1998, 84-year-old Rose Martin of Tiverton, Massachusetts, was buried in her 1962 Corvair. She'd bought it new for $2,500 and had decided she never wanted to be parted from it.

Roger Fox of Fairborn, Ohio, is a retired deputy sheriff who plans to be buried in his handmade coffin-car, assembled from two caskets and parts of various 1960s "muscle" cars. Meanwhile, he has something unique to drive around in.

Rose Martin was buried in her own car.

NOW

Verna Richardson, designer and president of Habco, Inc., makes caskets that look like 6-foot-long houses.

What a Way to Go!

Even if the coffin is plain, it doesn't mean the funeral has to be dull. In New Orleans, Louisiana, brass bands often accompany a funeral procession to the cemetery. On the way in, they play slow, mournful

Wynton Marsalis (center) plays the trumpet in bandleader Lionel Hampton's New Orleans–style funeral procession in New York.

music, but on the way out, they swing into such lively numbers as "When the Saints Go Marching In."

The Tombstone Hearse Company, with locations in four states, offers an alternative to traveling to the cemetery in a plain old Cadillac or Lincoln

Now motorcycle lovers can take their last ride to the cemetery in a hearse pulled by a modified Harley-Davidson trike.

hearse. Combining old-fashioned glass-sided hearses and converted Harley-Davidson motorcycles, the company will not only carry the deceased to the cemetery but also take him or her on a last ride past a favorite place or along a favorite road.

The Spreewald in Germany is an area made up of waterways that feed into the Spree River. For a winter funeral, the Wends people who lived there once put on their skates and pulled the casket, which was mounted on a sied, along the ice.

Last Resting Places

Sometimes being laid to rest doesn't turn out to be as peaceful as one might think. At the Paco Cemetery in Manila, Philippines, corpses are placed in chambers in the cemetery's wall for an annual rental fee—but if families fail to pay the fee, the remains are taken away and burned.

In the early days of New Orleans, Louisiana, bodies were buried in shallow graves because of the high water table. When it rained, the water table rose even higher, sometimes popping caskets right out of the ground. As a result, people began to entomb their loved ones aboveground in "Cities of the Dead." Poorer people are stashed in the walls, which consist of stacked-up vaults. Wealthier people have family tombs lined up in rows on either side of wide walkways.

In 1932, Robert Ripley inspected the Paco Cemetery in the Philippines.

Graves are sometimes dug up and moved to make way for highways or new construction. The Mount Moor Cemetery in West Nyack, New York, was not moved, but its peace is disturbed seven days a week as shoppers flock to the three-million-square-foot Palisades Center Mall, which was built around it.

Pet Places

In the United States alone, there are more than 600 pet cemeteries. Markers range from carved statues to stones incorporating a photograph of the deceased pet—or both.

Tombstones in the Mount Moor cemetery seem to watch as consumers drive in, getting ready to shop till they drop at the Palisades Center Mall.

Hartsdale Pet Cemetery in New York is the oldest active pet cemetery in the United States.

BEYOND RIP...

When you think of a tombstone, you probably picture a granite slab engraved with the name and dates of the deceased—and maybe the phrase "Rest in Peace." Not everyone, however, is quite so unimaginative. Here are some tombstones and epitaphs that won't soon be forgotten!

Here lies the body of Solomon Peas
Under the daisies and under the trees.
Peas not here—only the pod;
Peas shelled out; went home to God.
— Epitaph on a tombstone in Wetumpka, Alabama

A tractor-trailer is etched on the tombstone of a deceased trucker in the New Prospect Cemetery in Pine Bush, New York.

Here lies the body of dentist DeMille in the largest cavity he'll ever fill.
— Epitaph on a tombstone on Catalina Island, California

A cautionary tale for speeders, Jonathan Blake's tombstone near Uniontown, Pennsylvania, reads: *Here lies the body of Jonathan Blake/Stepped on the gas instead of the brake.*

Tombstones shaped like tall tree stumps can be found in the Westchester Hills Cemetery in Hastings-on-Hudson, New York.

Ashes to Ashes

Some people prefer to have their bodies cremated, or burned. The ashes, also called cremains, can be kept in an urn, buried, or scattered in a favorite place. For those who want to go out with a bang, however, Celebrate Life, a company in California, will scatter the deceased's ashes in a spectacular fireworks display launched from a barge called Heaven Sent. Themes include "Knocking on Heaven's Door," "Stairway to Heaven," and "When Irish Eyes Are Smiling."

Why scatter the ashes of a deceased loved one by hand when you can send them up in a colorful fireworks display?

Gone but Not Forgotten

At some point, everyone loses a beloved relative or friend to the grim reaper—but just because the loved one is dead doesn't mean he or she won't be missed. Mourning customs range from treasuring a keepsake made of "bone" china to severing one's own finger to mourn the death of a relative.

REMEMBER ME ALWAYS

In the past, people kept a lock of hair from a deceased loved one to carry in a locket or a ring. Today, a loved one can become the ring. When 80-year-old Edna MacArthur of Alberta, Canada, died in 2002, her family had her turned into a diamond and set in a gold ring! The transformation involves cremating the body and compressing it into a small cube. The cube is subjected to intense heat to convert it into carbon, then crafted into a synthetic diamond.

A loved one's ashes can be turned into a diamond.

Even if your loved one wanted his or her ashes scattered in the woods, you and other loved ones can still have a keepsake. Eternally Yours, a company in Biloxi, Mississippi, will incorporate just a small portion of the

Fred Reid was taken prisoner in France during the Battle of the Bulge in World War II. When he died in 1999, his family had Charles Krafft incorporate some of Reid's ashes into this hand-painted porcelain helmet. The rest are sealed inside.

ashes into paintings you can hang on your walls. Memory Glass of Santa Barbara, California, will suspend a handful of ashes in hand-blown glass spheres to display on tables or mantles. Another option is to have artist Charles Krafft of Seattle, Washington, use some of the ashes to make a Spone—human bone china—plate or figurine.

Masakichi (right) struck a similar pose to that of his lifelike wood statue (left) for these two 1896 photos.

PAINSTAKING MEMORIAL

When a woodcarver named Masakichi learned he was dying, he decided to leave a "living" image of himself to his beloved. He carved a statue of himself, then plucked the hair from every pore in his body and inserted each one in corresponding positions on the statue. He added his eyebrows and eyelashes and, for the finishing touches, pulled out his fingernails, toenails, and teeth, and attached them to the sculpture.

Ritual Mourning

Handprints of Hindu widows who committed suttee cover a wall of the Junagarh Fort in Bikaner, India.

Throughout time, people all over the world have devised rituals to express their grief at the death of a loved one. A ritual can be as simple as dressing in black clothing to as extreme as joining a husband in death. In India, tradition once required Hindu women to commit suttee, a ritual in which they threw themselves on their husband's funeral pyre. First, however, the women would leave the imprint of one hand in red pigment on a doorjamb. Before flinging themselves into the fire, royal wives whose husbands died in battle left their handprints on special walls, such as that near the main entrance to the Junagarh Fort in Bikaner, India.

Until recently, the Dani people (especially the women) of the Indonesian province of Irian Jaya cut off parts of their own body—usually a finger—to mourn the death of a relative. In Brazil, the Uape people of the Upper Amazon drank the ashes of their cremated dead mixed with casiri, a local alcoholic beverage, in the belief they would absorb all the good qualities of the deceased. As a sign of mourning, a widow of the Tikar people in Africa was required to wear two buttons from her deceased husband's clothing in her nostrils.

At Mount Minobu, Japan, Buddhists pay homage at the grave of Nichieren, founder of a Japanese sect, by allowing five candles to burn down to the flesh on each outstretched arm.

Faithful Companions

Mourning isn't limited to humans. Dogs have been known to go to great extremes when they've lost a beloved owner. When John Gray died in 1858, his Skye terrier, Bobby, stood watch over the grave in the old Greyfriars Churchyard in Edinburgh, Scotland, until he died 14 years later.

Robert Ripley stands beside the statue of Bobby erected outside the entrance to Greyfriars Churchyard.

In Japan, an Akita dog named Hachi always met the three o'clock train at Shibuya station so he could walk home with his owner, Eisaburo Ueno, a professor at Tokyo University. On May 25, 1925, Ueno didn't get off the train. He had died while at work. Relatives adopted Hachi, but the dog continued to meet the train every day until his death in 1935. Today, a statue of Hachi at the station commemorates the dog's faithfulness.

Out of the Grave

Not every body is buried or otherwise disposed of in one piece. Sometimes bodies or body parts find themselves in odd places or used in ceremonial rituals—like this 2,800-year-old Peruvian Moche Indian skull decorated with parrot feathers, copper eyes, and a ponytail.

The Incredible Shrunken Heads

The features on the face of the shrunken head at left are remarkably well preserved.

The Jivaro, a warlike people of the western Amazon River basin in South America, believed that to decapitate an enemy and possess his head was to keep for one's self all the powers of its original owner. For hundreds of years, the practice of head-shrinking was a closely guarded secret—but, somehow, Robert Ripley found out how it was done.

A Jivaro began the head-shrinking ritual by cutting off the head of his enemy as close to the torso as possible. He then slit the scalp from the crown of the head to the nape of the neck and carefully removed the skull. After sewing up the slit, the eyes, and the lips, he stretched the skin over a knob of wood and simmered it in boiling water and herbs just long enough for the skin to contract but not for the hair to fall out. When removed, the head was about two-thirds its original size.

Robert Ripley holds one of his prized shrunken heads.

To further shrink the head, the Jivaro dropped hot stones and sand inside and constantly turned it to heat it uniformly. Whenever the stones or sand began to cool, they were replaced. As the head dried and grew smaller, the Jivaro kneaded the features to help them retain their lifelike appearance. When the head was about the size of a baseball, the neck was sewn up.

The Jivaro thought that people could possess three souls: *nekas*, an ordinary soul; *arutam*, a soul acquired through drug-induced visions; and *miusak*, a soul to avenge the death of a murdered person. Since the *miusak* of a slain enemy was trapped inside the victim's shrunken head, or *tsantsa*, it could not take revenge against his killers.

A few of the shrunken heads in Ripley's extensive collection

FREAKY Forensics

Homicide detectives are able to solve a murder even after the victim has been dead for a very long time with the help of forensic scientists—people who study the processes a corpse goes through as it decays. The more scientists know about the effects of time, weather, and other factors on a corpse, the easier it is to determine when and how someone died. That's why forensic anthropologist Dr. William Bass started the Body Farm at the University of Tennessee. The only forensic lab of its kind, its three acres harbor dead bodies in various states of decay. Some are under leaves, some are in car trunks, and others are in shallow streams or under tarps. Where do they get the corpses? From people who donate their bodies to science.

The first thing you see when you enter the Forensic Museum in Bangkok, Thailand, is the museum's

William Bass studies a corpse left out on the ground at the Body Farm.

founder, Khun Songkran Niyomsane. Well, not him exactly—just his skeleton. Continue on and you will see an assortment of body parts, bleeding brains, skulls with bullet holes, severed arms with tattoos, and a set of lungs with stab wounds. In one room, a case of skulls shot at from a variety of angles by forensic scientists shows just how bullets ricochet inside brain cases. In another room are jars of diseased organs— grim examples for medical

The mummified body of a serial killer at the Forensics Museum in Bangkok, Thailand

students of what can go wrong with a human body. However, the main attraction by far is the mummy of Si Quey, a serial killer from the 1950s. Close inspection reveals an incision made by scientists who wanted to find out if a criminal brain looked any different from a normal one.

BODY ART

In the Czech town of Sedlec, thousands of people were buried in the cemetery of a monastery, many of them during the plague of the 14th century. Eventually, the cemetery filled up, and in 1511, the monks began digging the bones up and storing them in a chapel. In 1870, a woodcarver named Frantisek Rint was

hired to do something about them—and did he ever! Rint used the bones of 40,000 people to make everything from the bone altar with its bone chalice, to bone chandeliers, to a literal coat of arms.

In the 1700s, Honoré Fragonard, an anatomy teacher, obtained cadavers from veterinary schools, executions,

A chandelier in the Sedlec bone chapel is made from every bone in the human body.

medical schools, and even fresh graves. He then stripped them of skin, dissected all the muscles and nerves, injected the blood vessels with wax, and steeped the bodies in alcohol for days. Finally he stretched them into elaborate poses and dried them with hot air. The finished objects were bought by the very wealthy, among them, King Louis XV. Examples of Fragonard's work can still be seen in the Fragonard Museum in France.

Today, German professor Gunther von Hagens has created an elaborate public anatomy lesson with his traveling exhibit of donated human corpses in active poses, such as running and playing games. The bodies, minus their skin, are preserved by *plastination,* a process that involves replacing bodily fluids with plastics.

A plastinized corpse contemplates a chessboard.

STRAY BODY PARTS

Besides being used in rituals, body parts have occasionally been known to go missing. In the 1850s, the skull of philosopher and theologian Emanuel Swedenborg (1688–1772) was stolen from his casket. More than 100 years later it turned up at auction, and on March 6, 1978, the Royal Swedish Academy of Sciences bought the skull for $10,560 and returned it to Swedenborg's coffin.

When author Thomas Hardy died in 1928, his ashes were buried at Westminster Abbey in London, England—but not before the family cat stole his heart. It was later recovered and buried in Stinson, England.

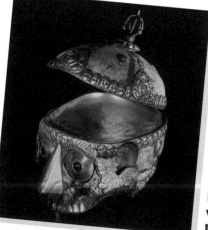

Sometimes unburied body parts are saved and become relics displayed in museums. The middle finger of the right hand of Galileo (1564–1642), astronomer and inventor of

In Tibet, Buddhist monks once drank out of bowls made from human skulls to remind worshipers of the temporary nature of life.

the telescope, can be seen at the Museum of the History of Science, in Florence, Italy.

In 1718, Edward Teach, a pirate known as Blackbeard was beheaded by British seamen during a battle off the North Carolina Coast. His head was placed on a stake at the mouth of the Hampton River as a warning to other pirates.

On the even more gruesome side is the book containing the transcript of the 1828 trial of convicted murderer William Corder—which is bound in his own skin. It can be seen on display in Moyses Hall Museum, Bury Saint Edmunds, England.

In 1998, a skull thought to be Blackbeard's was exhibited beside his portrait at the Mariners' Museum in Newport News, Virginia.

KEEPING WATCH

In his will, Jeremy Bentham (1748–1832), whose philosophy influenced the founding of the University of London (now University College London), left provisions that his body be made into what he called an "Auto-Icon," which eventually ended up at the University. After his body was dissected, his skeleton was dressed in his own clothes, topped by his mummified head, and seated in a wood

The "Auto-Icon" of Jeremy Bentham can be found in University College London.

cabinet. Since preservation of the head didn't go so well, a wax head was substituted, and the mummified head sat on the floor between his feet—at least until it was stolen and hidden by students one too many times.

Restless Spirits

You may not believe in ghosts, but there are lots of people all over the world who swear that they've seen or heard them. In some places, there are even celebrations to honor or appease the ghostly souls of the dead. So close your eyes for a few moments and enter into the spirited tales that follow.

Twilight Zone

In 1847, John and Margaret Fox moved their family into a house in Hydesville, New York, which was said to be haunted. In March 1848, the family began to hear strange noises, sometimes so loud they couldn't sleep. Finally, on March 31, Kate Fox, one of the daughters, snapped her fingers and dared whatever was making the noises to match her snaps. It did. Soon Kate and her sister Margaretta had worked out a way of communicating with the noisy spirit through raps indicating yes or no or a different letter of the alphabet. The spirit claimed to be a traveling salesman who'd been murdered and buried in the cellar by someone who'd

Austrian director Fritz Lang (1890–1976) captured all the spookiness of a séance in his 1922 film, *Dr. Mabuse, der Spieler*, about a hypnotist who was also a master criminal.

Thomas Edison, inventor of the lightbulb and many other devices, was also interested in the psychic world. In fact, he invented (but never patented) a machine for communicating with the dead.

COPYRIGHT BY THOMAS A. EDISON

previously lived in the house. Eventually, they learned his name was Charles B. Rosna. When the ground was soft enough, digging revealed what might have been some human hair and bones. Regardless, the Fox sisters soon became known far and wide for their ability to communicate with spirits. What about the murdered traveling salesman? In 1904, a wall in the Fox house collapsed, revealing a human skeleton. Whether or not the bones belonged to Rosna has never been proven.

After the Fox sisters' story got out, many Americans got caught up in the spiritualist movement. In the belief they could communicate with the dead, men and women called mediums held séances. In a séance, a group of people sat at a table, sometimes holding hands, in a darkened room. The medium would go into a trance and summon the spirits of deceased loved ones. If spirits were present, the attendees might see the table tilt, hear loud raps, or see strange lights. Eventually, many mediums were shown to have faked these special effects.

Spirited CELEBRATIONS

According to Chinese tradition, the ghosts of the dead return to Earth to visit their relatives during Ghost Month. At the Keelung Ghost Day Festival in Taiwan, lanterns on top of bamboo poles as tall as 10 feet are used to call the ghosts to a feast, and water lanterns are released in Wanghai Harbor to lure the water spirits.

Every May, the Bun Festival is held on the island of Cheung Chau, near Hong Kong. The festival began hundreds of years ago as a ceremony to lay to rest the ghosts of people who had died in a terrible storm or during an outbreak of the plague. On the last day of the festival, thousands of fresh, warm buns are attached to three 52.5-foot-tall towers in front of the Pak Tai Temple to appease the spirits—and later eaten by the attendees.

Every five years or so in

Water lanterns in Wanghai Harbor during the Keelung Ghost Day Festival

Madagascar, people observe Famadihana, when they honor their dead loved ones with a sumptuous feast in the hope it will bring the family good fortune. The families remove their dead relatives from their tombs, bring them up-to-date on family news, and even dance with the dead bodies before sitting down to a lavish banquet. Afterward, the bodies are given new shrouds and returned to their tombs.

The Phi Ta Khon festival takes place every June in Dan Sai, Thailand, to commemorate the return of Buddha in his next-to-last incarnation. It's said that even the village spirits took part in the welcoming parade on this joyous occasion.

Village men dressed up as spirits at the Phi Ta Khon festival.

Ghostly Royalty

The Tower of London, built by William the Conqueror in 1066, in London, England, is famous for its former function as a prison and execution site. The Tower is equally famous for being haunted by the souls of its dead prisoners, such as the murdered King Henry VI; the beheaded Anne Boleyn, second wife of King Henry VIII; and Lady Jane Grey, who was beheaded at the age of 17 for high treason.

The Tower of London at night

Fatal Forebodings

Sometimes people get advance warning of their own or someone else's death through dreams or visions, or from a psychic. An author may even unwittingly write a book that foreshadows a grim future. Being forewarned, however, doesn't necessarily mean death can be avoided.

Some people have dreams or visions that tell them how and when they or a loved one will die. President Abraham Lincoln (1809–1865) told several people that in a dream, he'd seen a coffin lying in state in the East Room. When he asked who had died, he was told, "The president. He's been assassinated." Not long afterward, Lincoln was killed by an assassin's bullet.

DREAMS
AND VISIONS

One March night, the wife of Julius Caesar (100–44 B.C.E.), ruler of Rome, dreamed that a statue of her husband was dripping with blood. The morning of March 15, she warned him not to go to the senate.

Abraham Lincoln was shot by John Wilkes Booth on April 14, 1865, and died the next day.

Caesar refused to listen—and was stabbed to death by senators who feared he was becoming too powerful.

The poet William Blake (1757–1827) quit his job the first day that he was apprenticed to William Rylands, England's foremost engraver. The reason? When Blake looked at his employer, he had a chilling vision of Rylands hanging dead on a gallows. Twelve years later, Blake's vision came true when Rylands was hanged for forgery.

Julius Caesar's wife, Lydia, dreamed he was in danger and begged him not to go to work on the day he was assassinated.

Not everyone who has a dream foretelling a death is famous. At five o'clock on the morning of November 2, 1951, Nova Churchill woke up crying, "I dreamed a black panther jumped on my mother and killed her." A phone call received later that day confirmed Churchill's dream. Her mother had had a heart attack while dusting a ceramic panther—at the exact moment Churchill awoke from her dream.

Dire Predictions

Psychics seem to have a sixth sense that makes them especially sensitive to people and their surroundings. Psychic Jeanne Dixon (1918–1997) was on her way to give a speech at the Ambassador Hotel in Los Angeles, California, in 1968. As she passed through the kitchen to get to the room where she was to speak, she stopped suddenly and blurted, "This is the place where Robert

Rasputin was poisoned, shot several times, then tossed into the Neva River—where he finally drowned!

Kennedy will be shot. I can see him being carried out with blood on his face." Not long afterward, her prediction came true.

Some people's predictions seem confined to their own death. The day before he was killed, the Russian monk Grigory Rasputin (1872–1916) wrote a letter in which he correctly predicted his own murder.

Halley's comet

In 1897, a reporter showed Mark Twain a cablegram from the *New York Journal* suggesting that Twain had died. Twain responded to the newspaper saying, "The report of my death was exaggerated."

can be seen from Earth only once every 75 years. When Samuel Langhorne Clemens, also known as Mark Twain, was born in 1835, the comet could be seen in the sky. Clemens said that just as he had come in with the comet, he would go out with it. The comet returned in April 1910—and Clemens died on April 21.

Instead of words, Arnold Dobler of Neustadt, Germany, predicted death with his actions. For 38 years, he always dug a new grave—exactly 24 hours before the death of a fellow parishioner!

Novel Prediction

A scene from Director James Cameron's 1997 movie *Titanic*, which won 11 Academy Awards, including Best Picture.

Futility, an 1898 novel by Morgan Robertson (1861–1915), was about the maiden voyage of the *Titan,* an 800-foot-long ocean liner that was said to be unsinkable. Carrying 3,000 people, the ship left England for New York in April, but one night near midnight, it struck an iceberg on its starboard side and sank. There weren't enough lifeboats for everyone aboard, and most perished in the icy waters of the North Atlantic.

In 1912, the *Titanic,* an 882-foot-long ocean liner was said to be unsinkable. Carrying 3,327 people, the ship left England on its maiden voyage for New York in April, but one night at 11:40 P.M., it struck an iceberg on its starboard side and sank. There weren't enough lifeboats for everyone aboard, and 1,523 perished in the icy waters of the North Atlantic. Did Robertson foresee the sinking of the *Titanic,* or was his story simply a coincidence?

Deathly
Coincidences

When you experience a strange coincidence, do
you think it's just chance? Or do you believe it
was fated to happen and has some deeper,
mysterious meaning you can
only guess at? Whichever you
believe, see if you feel the
same way after reading
about the following
creepy coincidences.

Seriously Creepy!

Two of America's most beloved presidents, Abraham Lincoln and John F. Kennedy, are linked by an eerie set of coincidences. A pattern runs through the circumstances of their presidencies and assassinations that hints at some unknown, unexplained connection.

Abraham Lincoln (1809–1865)

☠ Both Kennedy and Lincoln were deeply involved in the civil rights issue of his era. In Lincoln's time, the issue was slavery; in Kennedy's, it was segregation.

☠ Lincoln's assassin, John Wilkes Booth, was born in 1839. Kennedy's assassin, Lee Harvey Oswald, was born in 1939.

☠ Lincoln had a secretary named Kennedy who warned him not to go to the theater that night. Kennedy had a secretary named Lincoln who warned him not to go to Dallas, Texas.

- ☠ Both Lincoln and Kennedy were shot on a Friday.
- ☠ Both were shot from behind.
- ☠ Both wives were present when their husbands were shot.
- ☠ Booth shot Lincoln in a theater and ran into a warehouse. Oswald shot Kennedy from a warehouse and ran into a theater.
- ☠ Both presidents were succeeded by men named Johnson.
- ☠ Both Johnsons were Democrats from the South.
- ☠ The Johnson who succeeded Lincoln was born in 1808. The Johnson who succeeded Kennedy was born in 1908.
- ☠ Both presidents' last names have seven letters. Their successors' first and last names combined have 13 letters, and the first and last names of their assassins have 15 letters.

John F. Kennedy and his wife, Jacqueline, arriving in Dallas, Texas, on November 22, 1963, just hours before he was assassinated.

CURSES!

Weighing in at 45.52 carats, the Hope Diamond is not only the largest deep blue diamond in the world but also one of the most cursed jewels—at least according to Pierre Cartier. Is it really? Well, Cartier was trying to sell the stone to Evalyn Walsh McLean, so perhaps he

exaggerated a bit. Nevertheless, the diamond was once owned by Louis XVI of France, who was beheaded with his wife, Marie Antoinette, in 1793. The diamond, along with other crown jewels, was stolen.

In 1822, the stone appeared in a portrait of George IV of England, a gambler and big spender who was deeply in debt when he died. Next, it was owned by Henry Philip Hope, for whom the stone is named, and passed down through his family until a descendant sold it to a jeweler to pay his debts. Six years later, in 1908, the Hope Diamond was bought by Sultan Abdul Hamid II of Turkey. The following year, the sultan was removed from power and sent into exile.

Cartier was the next owner, and his sales pitch worked. He sold it to Evalyn McLean in 1911. What happened then? In 1913, McLean's mother-in-law died; in 1919, her nine-year-old son was hit by a car and killed; in 1941, her husband died in a sanatorium; in 1946, her 25-year-old daughter died of a drug overdose; and one year later, McLean herself died. Were these misfortunes that might have been suffered by anyone or were they due to the ownership of the Hope Diamond? You decide.

In 1884, Walter Ingram returned to England with the mummified hand of an ancient Egyptian princess, which held a gold plaque that read, "Whoever takes me to a foreign land will die a violent death, and his bones will never be found!" Four years later, Ingram was killed by an elephant in Somaliland and buried in a dry riverbed. An expedition was sent to bring Ingram's body back to England, but it had been washed away by a flood.

On the last day of September 1955, movie star James Dean was driving his brand-new silver Porsche 550 Spyder to Salinas, California, to compete in a race. He never made it. Despite having already gotten a ticket for speeding, Dean was barreling down a hill on route 466 (now 46) at more than 80 miles per hour. Suddenly, a Ford pulled out of an intersection, and the two cars crashed head-on. Dean's passenger and the driver of the other car survived. Dean did not.

George Barris, who customized cars, bought the wrecked Porsche. While it was being unloaded in his garage, it fell on one of the mechanics and broke both his legs. Two doctors, Troy McHenry and William Eschrid, bought and installed parts from the Porsche in their own racecars. McHenry was killed when his car hit a tree, and Eschrid was seriously injured when his car

TROUBLE

flipped over. The two undamaged tires were sold to a man who was hospitalized after both tires blew out at the same time.

Barris loaned the wreck to the California Highway patrol to use in a traveling show about automobile safety. Not long afterward, a fire broke out in the garage where the Porsche was being stored, destroying every vehicle but the wreck. While on display in Sacramento, the car fell on a teenager, breaking his hip. The Porsche was once again bound for Salinas when the truck driver lost control, crashed, and was killed instantly.

In 1960, the Porsche was loaned to the Florida police for a safety display. The wreck was loaded onto a truck, but somewhere along the way, it disappeared, never to be seen again.

Brothers Erskine L. and Neville Ebbin of Bermuda died one year apart after being struck by the same taxi, driven by the same driver, and carrying the same passenger.

SCREEEEEE

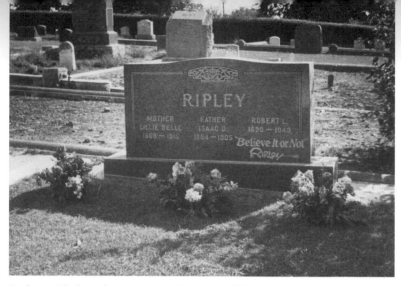

Robert Ripley shares a tombstone with his mother and father.

TAPPED
OUT

In a bizarre twist of fate Robert Ripley would have
appreciated, he had a heart attack and collapsed while
making the 13th episode of his weekly television series.
The segment Ripley had been filming was a dramatized
sequence on the origin of "Taps"—a hauntingly sad
tune played at military funerals. Three days later, on
May 27, 1949, Ripley died. He was buried next to his
parents in his hometown of Santa Rosa, California, in
a place called Oddfellows Cemetery.

Odds at the End

You've read about unusual burials and memorials, mourning customs and rituals, restless spirits, perilous predictions, and creepy coincidences. Now it's time to finish off with a few loony legacies, mysterious events, and strange superstitions.

SPECIAL BEQUESTS

Usually, people leave their money and belongings to their relatives, but occasionally, fortunes go to the dogs. Oil company heir Eleanor Ritchey, who died in 1968, left a 180-acre ranch in Deerfield Beach, Florida, plus $4,300,000 to 150 homeless dogs. When the last dog died in 1984, the estate, worth $12,000,000, went to a veterinary school.

John Reed, who was employed as a gaslighter at the Walnut Street Theater in Philadelphia, Pennsylvania, never missed a single performance in 44 years. When he died, he bequeathed his skull to the theater so that it could be used in the scene of William Shakespeare's play *Hamlet,* where the Danish prince picks up a skull in the graveyard and says, "Alas! Poor Yorick. I knew him . . ."

Playing the title role in *Hamlet,* Sarah Bernhardt (1844–1923) holds the skull of Yorick in the famous graveyard scene.

STRANGE Occurrences

Mysterious circumstances surround some deaths. For example, in World War I, a British observation plane on the western front flew in wide circles for several hours and then landed without mishap—even though its pilot and observer were both dead.

Burials, too, have had their share of uncanny events. The night before Queen Elizabeth I (1533–1603) of England was to be buried,

Before she became queen of England, Elizabeth I was imprisoned for a time in the Tower of London, where her mother, Anne Boleyn, had been beheaded by order of Elizabeth's father, King Henry VIII.

her casket mysteriously exploded. Though the coffin was destroyed, the queen's body was unharmed.

SUPERSTITIONS

England's King Charles II (1630–1685) rubbed the dust collected from Egyptian mummies on his skin in the belief that the greatness of the pharaohs would rub off on him.

Do you believe walking under a ladder, having a black cat cross your path, breaking a mirror, or spilling salt will bring bad luck? How do you feel about Friday the 13th?

Just about everybody is superstitious about something. Even if you don't believe in the bad luck ones, you probably make a wish when you blow out the candles on your birthday cake, right? Well, superstitions are nothing new. They've existed in every culture around the world for as long as humans have been around.

☠ In ancient England, burglars carried a mummified hand cut from the body of a hanged man in the belief that it could open locked doors.

- In Japan, it's customary for the family of a deceased person to hand out small packets of salt to mourners, since salt is believed to protect them from the ghosts of the dead.
- Many hotels in China don't label the fourth floor because the character for four in the Chinese written language is the same as the character for death.
- In Borneo, a human skull is placed between the bride and groom at weddings as a symbol that love can outlast death.

Many Hindus believe that if a sacred rat at the Karni Mata Temple in Rajasthan, India, accepts food from their hand, good luck will follow. The rats are believed to carry the souls of storytellers who will one day live again as humans.

Large bowls of milk and food are scattered throughout the Karni Mata Temple to feed the hundreds of sacred rats that live there.

Photo Credits

Ripley Entertainment Inc. and the editors of this book wish to thank the following photographers, agents, and other individuals for permission to use and reprint the following photographs in this book. Any photographs included in this book that are not acknowledged below are property of the Ripley Archives. Great effort has been made to obtain permission from the owners of all materials included in this book. Any errors that may have been made are unintentional and will gladly be corrected in future printings if notice is sent to Ripley Entertainment Inc., 7576 Kingspointe Parkway, Suite 188, Orlando, Florida 32819.